D0903313

Do wonderful things...

COBB - GRILL ON THE GO - 2009

Design & layout

www.toyplanet.co.za

Photography

Inga Hendriks (inga@mweb.co.za)

Recipe design & testing

David Grier (www.davidgrier.co.za)

Tamsyn Wells

Stylist

Tamsyn Wells

David Grier (www.davidgrier.co.za)

Taswell Mabutha (Assistant)

Location

Cassia Restaurant

Nitida Wine Farm

Durbanville, RSA

Publisher

Cobb International (Pty) Ltd

Registration number: 2000/000788/06

P.O.Box 68113, Bryanston 2021, South Africa

Phone: (+27 11) 463 1235

Fax: (+27 11) 463 1434

Email: cobb@cobbglobal.com

Website: www.cobbglobal.com

ISBN: 9780620435932

INTRODUCTION

The Cobb is a compact, portable outdoor cooking device. This kitchen in a bag gives you the ability to create dishes anywhere. The Cobb's advanced heating system is eco-friendly and energy efficient. Outdoor cooking is Cobbing!

THE COBB GRILL

The COBB Grill is made of only the highest quality durable materials and because the COBB has no moving parts, nothing can go wrong.

This highly portable grill weighs only 4kg (8.8lbs). The Cobb has a height of 35cm with the dome on (14 inches) and a length and width of 32cm (12.5 inches). Its stainless steel mesh base creates a heat shield with air pockets built-in, so it stays cool to the touch, and can be picked up or touched while cooking (a GREAT safety feature making it perfect for boating). You can cook on any surface... this is a true tabletop grill.

Use either the indicated amount of briquettes or a single Cobble Stone for over 2 hours of cooking.

The Cobb is very fuel efficient, using a single Cobble Stone or 8 - 10 charcoal briquettes (300grams / 10.6oz) for over 2 hours of cooking! The Cobb can be easily dismantled and cleaned. It is dishwasher safe and has a non stick surface for better cooking. The flow of air through the holes in the grill into the dome ensures an even cooking area, so that meat comes out both moist and crispy - this feature also makes the grill great for smoking.

ACCESSORIES

COBB DOME LID

The dome lid provides the Cobb with an all round function. Be it for cooking or baking. You can use the dome on almost every dish you cook as it isolates the heat inside and ensures an even spread of heat.

COBB FRYING DISH

Add even more versatility to your Cobb Cooking System with the Cobb Frying Dish - its heavy base construction provides an even, consistent cooking surface, perfect for cooking stews and curries, or a delicious healthy stir fry. Because it is constructed of stainless steel, you don't have to worry about rust, and it is tough enough to be used on your stovetop. Clean up is easy - just pop it in the dishwasher!

COBB FRYING PAN

The Cobb Pan takes grilling to a whole new level. The Cobb Pan has a heavy-duty base, creating an even cooking surface. Its non-stick coating means you can cook almost anything on your Cobb, from eggs, bacon and pancakes to pan-seared fish, quesadillas and pizza!

COBB GRIDDLE

NEW from Cobb is the Griddle Accessory. The grooved griddle sears burgers, steaks, sausage and veggies with a crosshatch pattern for healthy grilling. Grease and fat drains away from food and into the flavour moat leaving nothing but that delicious grilled taste. Non-stick surface makes for easy cleaning and is dishwasher safe.

COBB ROASTING RACK

The NEW Cobb Roasting Rack fits snugly above the standard Cobb Grilling Surface. The Roasting Rack eliminates the need to constantly flip chicken, ribs and roasts. Prevents searing and allows heat to circulate around the meat for the perfect slow roast.

Use the guide for choosing the accessories required for each recipe.

GRILLING TIPS

Make sure that the charcoal has burnt grey before you start the cooking process.

When cooking with the Cobble Stone, turn your roasts constantly as the Cobble Stone generates more heat than charcoal.

You can pour a cup of water, beer or wine into the moat of the Cobb when roasting. This adds moisture during the cooking process as well as helps to stop the fat burning during cooking.

Try to marinate the meats the night before to help tenderise and add flavour.

Allow the meat to reach room temperature before grilling to ensure even cooking.

Serve snacks before grilling so you can take your time cooking and the guests don't get hungry.

To prevent burning, soak kebab sticks in water before threading the meat on.

Foil is used with the shiny side inwards so the heat can penetrate the foil and will not be deflected.

Always heat the Cobb with the lid on and leave lid on during the cooking process to retain the heat.

Always remove the lid and the griddle after cooking. NEVER leave the lid on an empty Cobb.

To hold the juices inside after the cooking process always let the meat rest before carving.

APPETIZERS

VENISON

LAMB

BEEF

PORK

CHICKEN

FISH

VEGETABLES

KIDS

DESSERTS

BREAD

MARINADES & SAUCES

SALADS

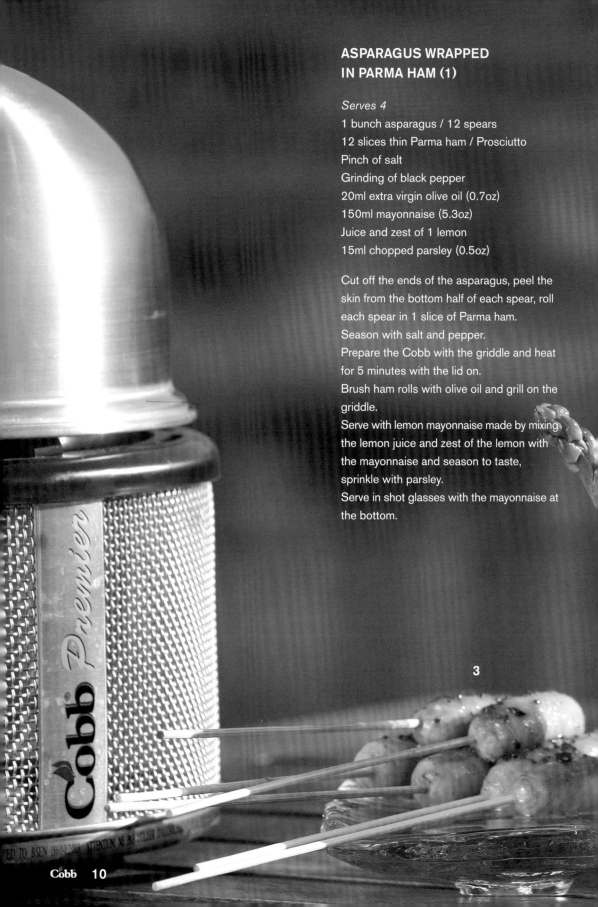

ASPARAGUS WRAPPED IN PARMA HAM (1)

Serves 4
1 bunch asparagus / 12 spears
12 slices thin Parma ham / Prosciutto
Pinch of salt
Grinding of black pepper
20ml extra virgin olive oil (0.7oz)
150ml mayonnaise (5.3oz)
Juice and zest of 1 lemon
15ml chopped parsley (0.5oz)

Cut off the ends of the asparagus, peel the skin from the bottom half of each spear, roll each spear in 1 slice of Parma ham.
Season with salt and pepper.
Prepare the Cobb with the griddle and heat for 5 minutes with the lid on.
Brush ham rolls with olive oil and grill on the griddle.
Serve with lemon mayonnaise made by mixing the lemon juice and zest of the lemon with the mayonnaise and season to taste, sprinkle with parsley.
Serve in shot glasses with the mayonnaise at the bottom.

3

BACON AND CHEESE GRILLER SKEWER (2)

Serves 4
4 cheese grillers (or any breakfast sausage)
1 packet streaky bacon (0.5lbs)
8 kebab sticks
5ml smoked paprika (0.1oz)
20ml olive oil (0.7oz)

Wrap cheese grillers in bacon spiralling from top to bottom.
Slice into 1.5cm thick slices.
Skewer 3-4 slices per kebab through the two bacon ends.
Mix the paprika and oil together and brush over the kebabs.
Prepare the Cobb with the griddle and heat with the lid on for 5 minutes.
These can be griddled or roasted on the Cobb until golden.

HONEY MUSTARD CHIPPOLATAS ON A STICK (3)

Serves 4
500g pork chippolatas (1.1lbs)
20ml oil (0.7oz)
100ml honey (3.5oz)
25ml wholegrain mustard (0.8oz)
Pinch of salt
Grind of black pepper
12-15 kebab sticks

Prepare the Cobb with the frying dish and heat for 5 minutes with the lid on.
Heat the oil in the frying dish attachment and begin browning the chippolatas.
Meanwhile mix the honey and mustard together.
Once the chippolatas start to colour, add the honey dressing and toss in the frying dish until golden and sticky.
Skewer the chippolatas onto a kebab stick and serve.

BRIQUETTES
x8

1

2

TOMATO, MOZZARELLA AND PESTO TOASTIES

Serves 4
8 slices bread/ciabatta
8 slices mozzarella/buffalo mozzarella
2 tomatoes, sliced
50ml basil pesto (1.7oz)

Butter the bread on the outside.
Place one slice mozzarella and
one slice tomato on one piece of bread.
Spread pesto on the other side and
sandwich together.
Prepare the Cobb with the griddle
plate and heat for 5 minutes with the
lid on.
Toast on the griddle until golden on both
sides.

LAMB KOFTAS WRAPPED IN BACON WITH TZATZIKI

Serves 4
500g minced lamb (1.1lbs)
1/2 cup coriander, chopped (4.3oz)
1/2 cup fresh mint, chopped (4.3oz)
1 teaspoon ground cumin (0.17oz)
1 teaspoon ground coriander (0.17oz)
1 small chilli, chopped
1 teaspoon turmeric (0.17oz)
5 ml dried cinnamon (0.1oz)

15ml pine nuts (0.5oz)
1 lime, zest and juice
1 large egg
1 cup fresh breadcrumbs
2 packets streaky bacon (1.1lbs)
Salt and pepper to taste
Skewers, soaked in water

Add the spices, crushed seeds and nuts to
the lamb mince as well as the turmeric, chilli,
fresh coriander, fresh mint, lime (zest and
juice) and a pinch of cinnamon and combine.

Add the egg and breadcrumbs.
Form the mince into balls and wrap in bacon.
Skewer three balls onto each stick.
Prepare the Cobb, place the frying pan on
and heat for 5 minutes with the lid on.
To cook, place the skewers on the frying pan
for 15 minutes with the lid on.

TZATZIKI

1 cup yoghurt (8.8oz)
1/2 cucumber, grated & squeezed to remove water
Juice and zest of 1 lemon
1 garlic clove, crushed
Salt and pepper

To prepare the tzatziki add the yoghurt, cucumber,
crushed garlic and lemon juice in a mixing bowl
and combine the ingredients together.
Add salt to taste.

BRIQUETTES x7

OSTRICH FILLET

Serves 4
800g ostrich fillet (1.8lbs)
10ml coriander seeds roasted and crushed (0.3oz)
Fresh coriander
2 garlic cloves
1 tablespoon soy sauce (0.5oz)
Salt and pepper
Olive oil

Marinate ostrich in olive oil, soy sauce, crushed coriander seeds and crushed garlic.
Prepare the Cobb with the griddle and heat with the lid on for 5 minutes.
Season the ostrich with salt & pepper and grill till medium rare.
Serve with roast tomato salsa and cucumber raita (pg79).

NAAN BREAD

550g flour (1.2lbs)
1/2 packet instant dry yeast (0.01lbs)
7ml salt (0.2oz)
100ml plain yoghurt (3.5oz)
50ml extra virgin olive oil (1.7oz)
200ml (7oz) tepid water - only add enough to make a soft dough.
Combine flour, yeast and salt and mix well.
Add the water, yoghurt and olive oil and combine to make soft dough.

Knead for 10 minutes.

Rest the dough in a warm place until doubled in size, knock down and let it rise again.
The dough is then ready to use.
Divide the dough into balls the size of golf balls and roll out on a floured surface.
Prepare the Cobb with the griddle and heat for 7 minutes with the lid on.
Brush the griddle with oil before placing the Naan bread on it.
Cook on the griddle until light brown on both sides.

BRIQUETTES x7

MARINATED QUAIL

Serves 4
4 whole quails
4 tablespoons olive oil (2.1oz)
4 tablespoons lemon juice (2.1oz)
4 tablespoons parsley (2.1oz)
1 tablespoon paprika (0.5oz)
1 tablespoon honey (0.5oz)
1 tablespoon hoisin or HP sauce (0.5oz)
2 tablespoons soy sauce (1oz)
2 cloves garlic chopped
Salt and pepper

Clean the quails. Tie the legs together with string.
Mix all of the ingredients into a marinade and brush onto the quail.
Prepare the Cobb using the roasting rack.
Place the quail on the roasting rack and roast with the lid on.
Turn and brush with the marinade regularly.
Cook for 30 minutes.
Serve with vegetable cous-cous.

VEGETABLE COUS-COUS

Serves 4
1 red pepper, seeded and diced
1 yellow pepper, seeded and diced
8 button mushrooms, finely chopped
1 small onion, chopped
1 clove garlic, chopped
Handful parsley, chopped
2 stalks spring onion
Juice of 1 lemon
50ml olive oil (1.7oz)
1 cup cous-cous (8.8oz)
1 cup boiling water (8.8oz)
Salt and pepper

Sauté the onion, peppers, mushrooms and garlic in the frying dish.
Pour the cous-cous over the boiling water, cover with a lid and leave for 5 minutes to swell.
Fluff up the cous-cous with a fork and add the vegetables, olive oil, lemon juice and seasoning.
Sprinkle with chopped parsley and spring onion.

OPTIONAL: chunky roast vegetables may also be added to the cous-cous in place of the onion and peppers.

Cobb

BRIQUETTES
x8

GRILLED VENISON LOIN (SPRINGBOK)

Serves 4
800g Springbok loin (1.8lbs)
or venison of your choice
80ml olive oil (2.8oz)
2 sprigs rosemary, chopped
2 cloves garlic, chopped
1 tablespoon juniper berries (0.5oz)

Clean the loin of any fat or connective tissue
(or get the butcher to do it for you).
Mix the other ingredients and marinate for a
minimum of 1 hour.
Prepare the Cobb using the frying pan and
heat it with the lid on for 5 minutes.
Season the loin and grill on the Cobb
for 8-10 minutes.
Serve with caramelised onion, corn on the
cob and some salads.

OPTION: use any other venison loin.

BRIQUETTES
x8

CORN CAKES

Serves 4
1 tin (410g) corn in brine (0.9lbs)
1 tin milk (using the corn tin to measure)
(0.9lbs)
1 tin flour (using the corn tin to measure)
(0.9lbs)
1 extra large egg
1 small onion chopped
1 clove garlic
1 handful parsley
Squeeze of lemon
Pinch of paprika

Rinse the brine off the corn.
Prepare the Cobb with the frying dish and
heat for 5 minutes with the lid on.
Lightly fry the onions, garlic and corn kernels
in the frying dish.
Mix all the other ingredients together and add
the fried corn.
Season and add the chopped parsley.
Remove the frying dish and place the frying
pan on the heat with a few spoons of sunflower
oil, keep the lid on for 5 minutes.
Gently fry spoonfuls in shallow oil using the
frying pan until golden on both sides.
Serve with game or chicken.

CARAMELISED ONIONS

Serves 4
1kg onions, thinly sliced (2.2lbs)
50ml oil (1.7oz)
1 cup red wine (8.8oz)
120ml red wine vinegar (4.2oz)
120ml brown sugar (4.2oz)
Salt and pepper

Prepare the Cobb using the frying dish, heat
for 5 minutes
Sauté the onions lightly in the frying dish and
add the other ingredients.
Cook until all the liquid has cooked away and
the onions are sticky.
Season with salt and pepper and add sugar
if necessary.
Goes well with all meats.

POTATO SALAD

Serves 4
800g potatoes (1.8lbs)
200ml mayonnaise (7oz)
2 spring onions
Handful parsley
Handful chives
6 gherkins
Pinch of sugar
Juice of 1/2 lemon
80ml milk (2.8oz)
Salt and pepper
3ml paprika (0.1oz)
2 boiled eggs, peeled and chopped or grated

Boil the potatoes in their skins, cool then
peel and cube.
Mix the other ingredients and pour over the
potatoes.
Season and sprinkle with paprika and chives.

GREEK-SPICED DEBONED
LEG OF LAMB

2kg leg of lamb, deboned (4.4lbs)
Handful coriander, chopped
Handful mint, chopped
Juice of 1 lemon
50ml olive oil (1.7oz)
5 cloves garlic, crushed
15ml coriander, ground (0.5oz)
15ml cumin, ground (0.5oz)
100ml Greek yoghurt (3.5oz)

Mix all ingredients together and rub over the
lamb and marinade over night.
Prepare the Cobb with the roasting rack, heat
with the lid on for 5 minutes.
Place in the Cobb and roast for 1 hour 40
minutes with the lid on. Turn every 15 minutes.
Remove from the Cobb and let it rest
for 10 minutes.
Place back in the Cobb and heat for 10
minutes, carve and serve with roasted
vegetables.

RACK OF LAMB

Serves 4
800g rack of lamb (1.8lbs)
80ml olive oil (2.8oz)
3 sprigs rosemary
15ml wholegrain mustard (0.5oz)
15ml lemon juice (0.5oz)
45ml red wine (1.5oz)
3 garlic cloves
Salt and black pepper

Clean the bones of the rack of lamb about 3cm (1.2 inch) from the end so the meat does not burn and trim excess fat from the loin.
Create marinade by adding chopped rosemary and garlic into the oil, lemon juice, red wine and mustard.
Marinade the lamb for a minimum of 30 minutes.
Prepare the Cobb using the roasting rack and heat for 5 minutes with the lid on.
Place the rack of lamb in the Cobb, cook with the lid on for 20 - 25 minutes.
Baste the lamb with the marinade and cook for a further 15 minutes.
Remove from the Cobb and let the rack of lamb rest for 5 minutes.
Cut and serve.

BABY JACKET POTATOES

Serves 4
12 new potatoes, 800g (1.8lbs)
Salt and pepper
Garlic butter
Chopped parsley
Tin foil

Par-boil the potatoes for 10 minutes (this is optional to speed up the process).
Wrap each potato in foil and bake on the roasting rack for 30 minutes with the lid on.
Make a criss cross slit in the foil and squeeze each potato gently exposing the soft potato centre.
Top with garlic butter, seasoning and fresh parsley.

BRIQUETTES x8

SEARED BEEF SALAD

Serves 4
800g Beef fillet (1.8lbs)
1 packet rocket leaves
15ml capers washed (0.5oz)
30g parmesan shavings (1oz)
Salt and pepper
20ml balsamic vinegar (0.7oz)
40ml olive oil (1.4oz)

Season and sear the fillet on the frying pan.
Cook with lid on for 10 minutes each side.
Let the fillet rest for 30 minutes.
Slice the cooked fillet in thin slices, top with
rocket, parmesan, capers and seasoning.
Mix the balsamic vinegar and olive oil together
and drizzle over the salad.
Eat with focaccia or garlic bread for a light
lunch.

BRIQUETTES
x7

WILD MUSHROOM SAUCE

Serves 4
150g Portabellini mushrooms, sliced (5.3oz)
80g Porcini mushrooms, sliced (2.8oz)
30g dried Porcini mushrooms, chopped (1oz)
1 small onion, chopped
2 cloves garlic, chopped
25ml brandy (1oz)
800ml cream (28.2oz)
Salt and pepper

Prepare the Cobb with the frying dish and
heat for 5 minutes with the lid on.
Fry the onion, garlic, Porcini and Portabellini
mushrooms in the frying dish.
Add the brandy and flambé.
Add the cream and cook slowly until reduced
and slightly thickened.
Mix any reserved meat juices from the
frying dish.
Season and serve with beef or chicken.

OPTION: the mushrooms can be replaced
with 2 tablespoons chopped green
peppercorns for a pepper sauce.

BRIQUETTES x8

BASIC GRILLED SIRLOIN STEAK

Serves 4
4 by 200g sirloin steaks (1.8lbs)
100ml BBQ sauce (3.5oz) (pg78)
2 sprigs rosemary
2 cloves garlic, chopped
Salt and pepper
30ml oil (1oz)

Brush steaks with the BBQ sauce and sprinkle
with oil, garlic, rosemary and seasoning.
Prepare the Cobb with the griddle and heat
for 5 minutes with the lid on.
Grill for 3 minutes on each side.
Serve with mushroom sauce.

FILLET

Serves 4
800g fillet (1.8lbs)
Salt and pepper
40ml olive oil (1.4oz)

Prepare the Cobb with the griddle and heat
for 5 minutes with the lid on.
Season and sear the fillet on the griddle.
Cook with lid on for 15 minutes each side.
Let the fillet rest for 30 minutes.
Slice the cooked fillet.
Eat with focaccia or garlic bread for a
light lunch.

GRILLED BEEF BURGER

Serves 4

600g lean beef mince (1.3lbs)
1 small onion, chopped
3 cloves garlic, minced
1 chilli, chopped
1 egg
3 slices of fresh bread, crumbed
80ml tomato sauce (2.8oz)
15ml Worcestershire sauce (0.5oz)
Squeeze of lemon juice
10ml sugar (0.3oz)
Salt and pepper
Handful parsley, chopped
Guacamole
8 slices crispy bacon

Prepare the Cobb with the frying pan.
Sauté the onion, garlic and chilli on
the frying pan.
Add the sauté to the mince with the other
ingredients, mix well and shape into 180g
(0.4lbs) beef burger patties.
Heat griddle plate with lid on for 5 minutes.
Brush with oil and grill burgers patties.
Serve on a hamburger bun with lettuce,
guacamole and crispy bacon.

OPTIONAL: add tomato slices and crispy
onion rings.
This can be made with pork, chicken, lamb or
ostrich mince.
You can make an ostrich burger with
mushroom sauce (pg26).

GUACAMOLE

Serves 4

1 large or 2 small avocados
30ml cream cheese (1oz)
30ml mayonnaise (1oz)
Juice of 1/2 lemon
Handful chopped coriander
1 sliced spring onion
1 tomato, seeds removed and cut into dice
Salt and pepper

Mash the avocado with a fork or blender
until smooth.
Add the mayonnaise, cream cheese, lemon
juice and coriander.
Season to taste and top with diced tomato's
and chopped spring onion.

OPTIONAL: use as a hamburger topping or
dip with chips.
Cook tortillas until crisp, top with cheese and
serve with guacamole, nacho style.

BRIQUETTES
x7

GRILLED LAMB KEBABS

Serves 4
500g lamb loin, cut into cubes (1.1lbs)
2 green peppers, cut into cubes
Dried apricots

MARINADE
2 garlic cloves, minced
Grinding of black pepper
1/4 tablespoon crushed peppercorns (0.04oz)
1/2 teaspoon salt (0.08oz)
3 tablespoons olive oil (0.5oz)
Juice of 1 lemon

Combine marinade ingredients.
Add the cubed lamb, mix well and marinate
for 1/2 an hour.
Divide the lamb into 4, thread onto a skewer
alternating the meat with apricots and peppers.
Prepare the Cobb with the roasting rack.
Grill on the Cobb for 15 minutes turning often and
brushing with the marinade as the kebabs cook.

OPTIONAL: any meat may be used for kebabs and
marinated with a marinade of your choice.

THREE BEAN SALAD

Serves 4
1 small onion, finely chopped
1 small green or red pepper, finely chopped
1 red chilli, chopped
3 tins of beans (410g) (0.9lbs), choose three bean
types (butter beans, red kidney beans, sugar beans,
baked beans, sliced green beans or chickpeas)
1 bunch fresh parsley, chopped

DRESSING
1/4 cup olive oil (2.2oz)
1/4 cup brown vinegar (2.2oz)
1/4 cup brown sugar (2.2oz)
Salt and pepper

Chop the vegetables and herbs.
Rinse the brine off all the beans (except the
baked beans).
Mix the dressing ingredients.
Mix the vegetables, herbs and beans.
Add together and chill for 2 hours.

BRIQUETTES
x8

SPARE RIB / CHICKEN WING MARINADE

2 tablespoons dry sherry (1oz)
2 tablespoons honey (1oz)
2 tablespoons light soy (1oz)
2 tablespoons sesame oil (1oz)
300ml tomato sauce (10.5oz)
1 red chilli
1/2 teaspoon five spice powder
(0.08oz)
1 teaspoon ground coriander (0.1oz)
1/2 teaspoon pepper (0.08oz)
100ml water (3.5oz)

Mix all ingredient in a bowl.
Marinate 2 kg (4.4lbs) pork ribs or
chicken wings.
Marinate for at least 4 hours
before using.

SMOKEY SPARE RIBS

Serves 4
1.2 kg lean spare ribs (2.6lbs)

MARINADE
1 cup tomato sauce (8.8oz)
150ml brown sugar (5.2oz)
35ml white vinegar (1.2oz)
30ml honey (1oz)
Splash of Worcestershire sauce
5ml salt (0.1oz)
10ml Dijon mustard (0.3oz)
2 chopped chillies
10ml smoked paprika (0.3oz)
1/2 minced onion
1-2 teaspoons liquid smoke (0.1oz)
2 minced garlic cloves
30ml tomato paste (1oz)
1 bunch spring onions

Prepare the Cobb with the frying dish to make
the sauce.
Combine the marinade ingredients together
in the frying dish and simmer for 10 minutes.
Remove the frying dish and replace with the
roasting rack to cook the ribs.
Brush the marinade over the ribs.
Grill slowly for 45 minutes basting constantly
and turning the ribs every 10 minutes.
To serve, cut the ribs into smaller pieces and
sprinkle with chopped spring onions.

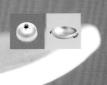

BACON WRAPPED PORK FILLET

Serves 4

800g pork fillet (4 pork fillets) (1.8lbs)
2 packets streaky bacon (1.1lbs)
10g fresh sage (0.3oz)
20ml olive oil (0.7oz)
Pinch of salt
Grind of pepper

Chop the sage and add to the olive oil.
Brush the oil over the fillet and season, then wrap in bacon spiralling from top to bottom.
Prepare the Cobb with the roasting rack and heat for 5 minutes with the lid on.
Cook slowly so as not to burn the bacon before the pork is cooked.
Remove the wrapped fillet, let it rest for 5 minutes, then carve each fillet into about 6 slices.
Serve with cabbage salad.

CABBAGE SALAD

Serves 4

2 cups (17.6oz) shredded cabbage or 1/4 head green/red cabbage or a mixture of both.
1 large shredded carrot
2 stalks chopped spring onion / 1/4 red onion
Handful chopped parsley
100ml creamy mayonnaise (3.5oz)
50ml prepared salad dressing, oil based (1.7oz)
Salt and pepper
10ml sugar (0.3oz)

Mix all the vegetables together.
Mix the parsley, mayonnaise, dressing and sugar.
Pour over the vegetables and season.

OPTIONAL: add 2 segmented oranges and a sprinkling of poppy seeds for a citrus flavour in place of the prepared dressing.

BRIQUETTES
x8

CARAMELISED APPLES

Serves 4
4 Granny Smith apples, peeled and cored
100g butter (3.5oz)
100g brown sugar (3.5oz)
Fresh sage

Prepare the Cobb with the frying dish.
Melt the butter in the frying dish and gently
fry the apples for 5 minutes.
Add the brown sugar.
Cook the apples until they are sticky and
cooked through.
Add chopped sage and serve with any pork
dish.

OPTION: this also makes for a fantastic dessert
with custard or ice cream.

ROAST PORK LOIN

Serves 4
1kg pork loin rolled and tied (2.2lbs)
15ml salt (0.5oz)
15ml olive oil (0.5oz)
5 sprigs rosemary
Sprig of sage
1 grinding of black pepper

Marinate the pork in olive oil, chopped sage
and chopped rosemary for 30 minutes.
Sprinkle with salt.
Prepare the Cobb with the roasting rack and
heat for 5 minutes with the lid on.
Roast the pork using the roasting rack for
about 1hour 45 minutes, 15 minutes
on each side
Rest the meat for 15 minutes and then slice.
Serve with caramelised apples.

SPICED PORK CUTLETS

Serves 4

4 x 200g pork cutlets (1.8lbs)
5ml ground black pepper (0.1oz)
5ml chilli powder (0.1oz)
20ml Worcestershire sauce (0.7oz)
5ml Dijon mustard (0.1oz)
1/2 tablespoon salt (0.26oz)
1/2 tablespoon ground cumin (0.26oz)
1/2 tablespoon smoked paprika (0.26oz)
2 garlic cloves, minced
50ml oil (1.76oz)

Mix all the ingredients together.
Rub the mixed ingredients all over the cutlets.
Leave to marinate for 1 hour.
Prepare the Cobb with the griddle and heat
for 5 minutes with the lid on.
Grill for 4 minutes a side on the Cobb griddle
(Make sure that you don't let the marinade
burn on the griddle. If it does, remove the pork
and wipe the burnt marinade off the griddle.
Replace and continue).
The cooking time should be about 15 minutes.
Serve with caramelised apples and
pasta salad.

ROAST TOMATO SALSA

800g plum tomatoes, cut in half lengthwise (1.8lbs)
1 medium onion, cut into six wedges
1 large garlic clove, halved
45ml extra virgin olive oil (1.5oz)
1 medium dried chilli, soaked in boiling water until
softened. Then drain off water
1/2 cup coriander, roughly chopped (4.4oz)
30ml red wine vinegar (1oz)
15ml olive oil (0.5oz)
12ml sugar (0.4oz)
Salt

Prepare the Cobb with the frying pan and heat with
the lid on.
Gently toss the tomatoes, onions, garlic and salt
with the olive oil in a large bowl.
After they are nicely coated arrange in a single layer,
tomatoes cut-side facing up, across a lined
baking sheet.
Roast in the Cobb for 25-30 minutes with the lid
on, or until the tomatoes start to collapse and the
onions begin to caramelize.
Remove from the Cobb.
Puree the chillies with the roasted garlic and two
roasted tomato halves. Chop the remaining tomatoes
by hand (once they've cooled a bit).
Chop and add the onions.
Season with salt and stir in the coriander.
Add the red wine vinegar, oil and sugar.

BRIQUETTES
x8

COBB PIZZA

Use 1 batch focaccia dough (pg49)

TOPPING
Tomato paste
Fresh basil, chopped
1 chilli
Sliced red pepper
Anchovies
Salami slices
Black olives
Mozzarella
Oregano

Roll the dough out to fit into the pan, making sure
that the dough is not more than 1/2 centimetre
thick (0.2inches).
Make the tomato sauce by mixing the paste with
basil, chilli and seasoning.
Spread over the dough and add the toppings.
Prepare the Cobb with the frying pan and heat
for 7 minutes with the lid on.
Place the pizza on the frying pan and cook for 15
minutes with the lid on.

OPTION: this pizza can be made with any topping
of your choice.

BRIQUETTES
x8

BACON AND MUSHROOM OMELETTE

(OPEN OR CLOSED)

Serves 4
8 eggs
15ml margarine/butter (0.5oz)
100ml milk/cream/water (3.5oz)
150g chopped crispy bacon (5.3oz)
100g sliced fried mushrooms (3.5oz)
50g mozzarella (1.8oz)
Chopped fresh chives
Salt and pepper

Whisk the eggs with the milk and
some seasoning.
Prepare the Cobb with the frying pan.
Melt the butter in the frying pan, add the eggs
topped with the bacon, grated mozzarella
and mushrooms.
Cook with the lid on until the egg is set.
Remove from the Cobb and sprinkle with
chives or fold the omelette in half for
a closed one.
Serve with chippolatas and grilled tomato.

BRIQUETTES
x7

WHOLE ROAST CHICKEN

Serves 4
1 whole chicken (±1.4kg / 3lbs)
50ml olive oil (1.7oz)
15ml salt (0.5oz)
10ml chicken spice (0.3oz)
1 lemon
4 sprigs rosemary
Ground pepper

Clean the chicken.
Make a dressing with the juice of the lemon,
olive oil, 2 sprigs chopped rosemary and
chicken spice.
Rub dressing all over the chicken & sprinkle
with ground pepper.
Place the lemon in the carcasse with 2 sprigs
of rosemary.
Prepare the Cobb with the roasting rack.
Grill the chicken for 1 hour with the lid on.
Turn every 10 minutes.
Cut up and serve.

CORN ON THE COBB

Serves 4
4 corn on the cob
4 cloves garlic
100g butter (3.5oz)
Handful chopped parsley
15ml sweet chilli sauce (0.5oz)
Salt and pepper

Mix the garlic, butter, parsley, chilli sauce and
seasoning together.
Par cook the corn in water (this is optional,
to speed up grilling time).
Prepare the Cobb with the griddle plate, heat
for 5 minutes with the lid on.
Lightly grill the corn on the griddle plate.
Spread the butter over the corn and
grill until browned.

BRIQUETTES
x9

STICKY CHICKEN DRUMSTICKS

Serves 4
8 chicken drumsticks / 16 chicken wings
Toasted sesame seeds
1 Spring onion, chopped

MARINADE
1/2 cup soy sauce (4.4oz)
15ml fresh ginger, minced (0.5oz)
15ml garlic, chopped (0.5oz)
5ml tom yum paste (0.1oz)
45ml sunflower oil (1.5oz)

GLAZE
1/2 cup honey (4.4oz)
1 1/2 tablespoons (0.8oz) Hoisin sauce or plum
sauce or HP sauce

Mix the marinade ingredients together, pour over the
chicken and leave for 1 hour.
Mix the glaze and set aside.
Prepare the Cobb with the roasting rack.
Grill chicken for 30 minutes turning constantly until
golden and just cooked.
Using a brush glaze the chicken while grilling until
the glaze caramelises (about 5-7 minutes).
Sprinkle with sesame seeds and spring onions.

BRIQUETTES
x8

BUTTERFLIED CHICKEN

Serves 4
1.5kg (3.3lbs) chicken butterflied (spatchcock)
Salt and pepper
50ml olive oil (1.7oz)
Juice of 1 lemon
4 cloves garlic crushed
50ml chopped thyme (1.7oz)
2ml cayenne pepper (0.07oz)
10ml paprika (0.3oz)

Use a spatchcock chicken or slice through
the back bone of a chicken and flatten it
yourself.
Mix the other ingredients together and rub
over chicken.
Let it marinate for 1 hour.
Prepare your Cobb with the roasting rack.
Cook in the Cobb with the lid on for 45-60
minutes, basting with the marinade.
Cut up and serve.

BRIQUETTES
x8

PASTA SALAD

Serves 4
400g fusilli pasta (0.8lbs)
200ml mayonnaise (7oz)
1 Granny Smith apple, cubed
10 mange tout pods, julienned
1 corn on the cob, cooked and
cut off the cob
2 peppadews, chopped
1/4 onion, chopped
3ml mild curry powder (0.1oz)
20ml chutney (0.7oz)
Handful coriander, chopped
Salt and pepper

Cook the pasta al dente.
Add the cubed apple, julienned mange tout,
chopped peppadew and corn removed
from the cob.
Fry the onion in a little oil, once soft add the
curry powder and mix this with the mayonnaise,
coriander and chutney.
Toss this with the pasta, season to taste and
top with fresh coriander leaves.

FOCACCIA

15ml dried yeast (0.5oz)
Pinch of sugar
450ml warm water (15.8oz)
750g strong white / bread flour (1.6lbs)
2 teaspoons salt (0.35oz)
75ml olive oil (2.6oz)
Toppings of your choice (potato, olives,
peppadews, caramelised onion)
Rosemary sprigs
Extra virgin olive oil

Dissolve the yeast and sugar in half the warm
water.
Leave for 10 minutes.
Mix the flour and salt and pour in the yeast
and olive oil.
Add the rest of the water and knead, then
allow to rise to double in size in a covered
bowl rubbed with olive oil.
Knock back and press into the Cobb frying
pan with your fingertips.
Brush with virgin oil and sprinkle with chopped
rosemary.
This can be topped with olives, roast peppers,
caramelised onions, garlic, cheese, tomato.
Prepare the Cobb.
Place the bread on the frying pan when it
is cold and then place it on the Cobb with
the lid on.
Cook in the Cobb for 10-12 minutes.

CHICKEN TORTILLA WRAP

Serves 4
4 tortilla wraps
600g chicken (1.3lbs)
4 tomatoes, skinned, pipped and cut into
blocks
1 red pepper, chopped
1 red onion, chopped
2 spring onions, chopped
60ml red wine vinegar (2oz)
15ml olive oil (0.5oz)
10ml sugar (0.3oz)
Salt and pepper
1 small packet mixed lettuce
125ml mayonnaise (4.2oz)
Handfull of coriander, chopped
200ml sweet chilli sauce (6.7oz)

Griddle or smoke the chicken (as per duck
recipe, pg53) and slice thinly.
Griddle one side of the tortilla.
Make a salsa by mixing the tomato, red pepper,
red onion, spring onion and coriander with
the vinegar, olive oil, sugar and seasoning.
Spread the mayonnaise over half of the
ungriddled side of the open tortilla.
Place lettuce evenly and top with chicken and
salsa.
Roll the tortilla into a tight cigar.
Place back on the griddle for a few minutes
to heat through.
Cut and serve with sweet chilli sause.

OPTIONAL: For an alternative use beef,
vegetables, salad, fish or game as a filling.

SMOKED DUCK BREAST

Serves 4

4 duck breasts

2 tablespoons coarse salt (1oz)

1 tablespoon fresh rosemary, chopped (0.5oz)

1/2 teaspoon pepper, crushed (0.08oz)

50g Smoke dust (1.7oz)

2 teabags

2 oranges

Score the fat on the breasts by cutting angular incisions into the fat.

Mix the salt, rosemary and pepper.

Coat the duck with the salt mixture and let it cure for 30 minutes.

Rinse the salt from the duck under running water.

Place the smoke dust and opened tea bags in an open foil pouch on the coals (Once the coals have turned grey).

Place the duck breast on the rack, skin side down and the lid on, smoke for 10-15 minutes.

If the fat has not rendered enough it can be cooked more on the griddle.

Serve with grilled orange slices made by using the griddle pan attachment.

OPTION: hot smoked salmon can also be made by replacing the duck with a Norwegian salmon fillet. Smoke this for 15 minutes.

BRIQUETTES x7

SWEET CHILLI PRAWNS

Serves 4
1kg prawns (+-21-25 prawns) (2.2lbs)
1 lemon
100ml sweet chilli sauce (5.5oz)
15ml olive oil (0.5oz)
Salt and pepper
Handful of coriander
2 tablespoons butter (1oz)

Remove the heads from the prawns and cut
down the back butterfly style.
Mix all the ingredients, sweet chilli sauce, olive
oil, lemon juice.
Pour over the prawns and let this marinate
for 10 minutes.
Prepare the Cobb with the frying pan and
heat for 5 minutes with the lid on.
Divide the prawns into 3 batches, melt some
butter on the frying pan and grill the prawns
in batches.
Grill for 1 1/2 minutes a side.
Then remove and do the next batch.
When you have finished, place all the prawns
on the frying pan, pour the remaining marinade
over them and heat for 2 minutes with
the lid on.
Season to taste and sprinkle with
coriander leaves.
This can be eaten as a snack before the
barbeque or with salads and potato as
a main course.

BRIQUETTES x8

SEARED TUNA BURGER, WASABI MAYONNAISE AND PICKLED CUCUMBER

Serves 4

4 thick tuna steaks 150g-180g each (0.3lbs)
2 tablespoons extra virgin olive oil (1oz)
15ml toasted sesame oil (0.5oz)
5ml salt (0.1oz)
1/4 tablespoon freshly ground black pepper
(0.13oz)
1 cup mizuna leaves or mixed lettuce (8.8oz)
4 hamburger buns
60ml pickled ginger (2.1oz)
200ml mayonnaise (7oz)
Squeeze of wasabi paste
1 handful coriander
100ml white wine vinegar (3.5oz)
15ml sugar (0.5oz)
3/4 cucumber, thinly sliced or peeled into ribbons

Brush steaks with olive oil, sesame oil and season
with salt and pepper.
Cut the top off the bun.
Top the base of the bun with mizuna
or mixed lettuce.
Prepare the Cobb with the frying dish, lid on and
pre-heat.
Bring the vinegar and sugar to the boil in the
frying dish then pour this over the cucumber slices,
season and let them cool.
Place the griddle plate on the Cobb and heat for
5 minutes with the lid on.
Sear the tuna steak on the griddle plate for 2
minutes a side.
Place on top of the mizuna leaves, top with pickled
cucumber and wasabi mayonnaise.
Serve with pickled ginger on the side.

BRIQUETTES
x7

FISH BAKED IN A PAPER OR FOIL POUCH (FISH EN PAPILOTTE)

Serves 4

800g fresh fish (1.8lbs)

1 packet baby vegetables with corn, carrots and mange tout

1 red pepper

1 packet egg/rice noodles

50g butter (1.7oz)

50ml soy sauce (1.7oz)

Handful coriander

400ml white wine or sake (14oz)

Cut 30cm (12inch) circles from foil or baking paper (x4).

Julienne the vegetables cutting into fine strips.

Cook the noodles, toss with the vegetables and season with soy sauce.

Divide the noodles and vegetables between the 4 paper or foil pouches.

Divide the fish into 4x200g (4x0.4lbs) portions.

Place the fish, butter and then the coriander on top of the vegetables.

Lastly add wine to each pouch (100ml) (3.5oz).

Prepare the Cobb with the roasting rack and pre heat.

Seal the foil or paper pouch by rolling the edges over, bake for 15-20 minutes on the roasting rack with the lid on.

BRIQUETTES x8

ROAST VEGETABLES IN A FOIL POUCH

Serves 4

600g (1.3lbs) cubed vegetables of your choice
(butternut, baby marrow, carrot, aubergine, peppers...)
80g butter (2.8oz)
2 sprigs rosemary/thyme
3 cloves garlic
Salt and pepper
Chopped fresh parsley
Tin foil

Tear a large double layer foil sheet.
Lie the vegetables in the centre.
Dot with butter, herbs, garlic and seasoning (close
pouch).
Place the pouch on the roasting rack for 45 minutes
with the lid on, turning often.
This can be added to cous-cous salad, eaten as a
side vegetable or rolled in a tortilla.
Make individual vegetable pouches
that can be eaten cold with
a salad dressing,
rocket leaves
and feta.

BRIQUETTES
x7

GRILLED SALMON WITH AN ORANGE SOY GLAZE

Serves 4
4 x 180g (0.4lbs) Norwegian salmon fillets

SPICE MIXTURE
1 tablespoon sugar (0.5oz)
1 tablespoon five spice powder (0.5oz)
1 tablespoon coriander, ground (0.5oz)
1 tablespoon black pepper (0.5oz)
1/2 tablespoon salt (0.26oz)

GLAZE
1/4 cup fresh orange juice (2.2oz)
1/2 cup low sodium soy sauce (4.4oz)
1/3 cup honey (2.9oz)
2 tablespoons spring onion, finely chopped (1oz)
1 piece fresh ginger, grated
1/2 tablespoon sesame oil (0.26oz)
2 garlic cloves, minced

Mix the spice ingredients together.
Mix all the glaze ingredients together.
Prepare the Cobb with the frying dish and pre-heat with the lid on.
Bring the glaze ingredients to the boil and simmer for 6 minutes in the frying dish.
Rub the salmon with the spice mixture, "spray and cook" the griddle plate and heat it on the Cobb with the lid on for 5 minutes.
Grill the salmon, skin side down first basting with the glaze for 4-6 minutes.
Turn the fish and cook on the flesh side for 4 minutes.
Serve this with the Nicoise salad.

LEMON, PARSLEY AND GARLIC NEW POTATOES (NICOISE)

Serves 4
550g new potatoes (1.2lbs)
Handful flat leaf parsley, chopped
1 lemon, zested
2 cloves garlic, crushed
Olive oil
125ml black olives (4.3oz)
100g cherry tomatoes, halved (3.5oz)

Boil the potatoes for 15-20 minutes (peeling is optional).
Toss in a pan with the other ingredients and season.
Serve with Norwegian salmon.

OPOTION: green beans, asparagus, wholegrain mustard and boiled egg can all be added to this dish.

WHITE WINE MUSSELS

Serves 4
1kg fresh mussels (2.2lbs), cleaned (remove
the beard) and scrubbed
3 large spring onions
1/2 onion, peeled and chopped
2 fat garlic cloves, peeled
1 fresh red chilli
Handful flat-leaf parsley
+-150ml dry white wine (5.2oz)
2 tablespoons crème fraiche/fresh cream
(1oz)
1/2 lemon
2 tablespoons olive oil (1oz)

Prepare the Cobb with the frying dish and
heat for 7 minutes, lid on.
Add olive oil and sauté the onions, garlic, and
chilli for 3 minutes.
Bring the wine to the boil with the onions,
garlic and chilli.
Add the mussels and the cream.
Place the lid on and steam in its own juices
until the mussels are open.
Discard any that did not open.
Top with roughly chopped parsley and a
squeeze of fresh lemon juice.

GARLIC BUTTER

500g block of butter (1.1lbs)
1 head garlic, peeled and crushed
15ml lemon juice (0.5oz)
Black pepper grinding
Handful chopped parsley

Soften butter and add garlic, parsley,
lemon, seasoning.
Use as a sauce for grilled meats, on potatoes,
on garlic bread and to sauté vegetables.

GARLIC BREAD

Serves 4
1 French loaf
150ml butter, softened (5.2oz)
4 garlic cloves
30ml parsley, chopped (1oz)
Squeeze of lemon
Grind of black pepper

Divide the French loaf into 2 or 3 depending
on the size so that it will fit into the Cobb.
Cut the French loaf 3/4 way down in slices
at intervals of 1.5cm (0.6inches) from the one
end to the other.
Chop the garlic finely and add to the softened
butter with the parsley, lemon and some
black pepper.
Spread the butter in each slit, wrap the loaf
in tin foil and bake in the Cobb on the roasting
rack for 15 minutes.

OPTIONAL: slices of tomato and mozzarella
may also be placed in each slit and serve with
fresh basil pesto.

BRIQUETTES
x7

ROCKY ROAD CHOCOLATE BARS

Makes 1 pan full (23cm/9.1in)
360g dark chocolate, chopped (12.7oz)
135g butter (4.8oz)
50ml golden syrup (1.7oz)
1 packet Marie biscuits or Tennis biscuits,
roughly crushed
110g mini marshmallows (3.9oz)
50g chopped toasted almonds (1.8oz)

Prepare the Cobb using the frying dish.
Slowly melt the butter in the dish with the
chocolate and syrup, mixing continuously.
Remove half a cup of the mixture.
Remove from the heat, add the biscuits,
marshmallows and nuts.
Transfer into a small rectangular dish.
Smooth into the dish and top with the other
half a cup of the chocolate mix.
Allow to set for 2 hours in the refrigerator.
Cut the set mixture into small slices and serve.

BRIQUETTES
x7

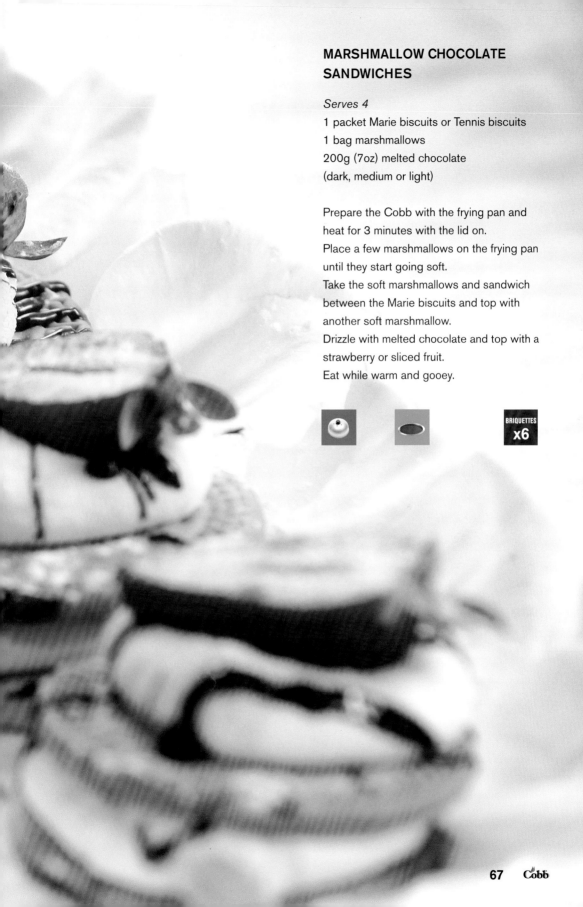

MARSHMALLOW CHOCOLATE SANDWICHES

Serves 4
1 packet Marie biscuits or Tennis biscuits
1 bag marshmallows
200g (7oz) melted chocolate
(dark, medium or light)

Prepare the Cobb with the frying pan and
heat for 3 minutes with the lid on.
Place a few marshmallows on the frying pan
until they start going soft.
Take the soft marshmallows and sandwich
between the Marie biscuits and top with
another soft marshmallow.
Drizzle with melted chocolate and top with a
strawberry or sliced fruit.
Eat while warm and gooey.

BRIQUETTES x6

GRILLED FRUIT AND MARSHMALLOW FONDUE

Serves 4
200g chocolate (7oz)
250ml cream (8.8oz)
1 packet marshmallows
1 punnet strawberries
1 bunch bananas peeled and cut into chunks
1 pineapple peeled and cut into chunks

Skewer the strawberries with the marshmallows.
Skewer the pineapple with the banana.
Prepare the Cobb with the frying dish and heat for
5 minutes with the lid on.
Melt the chocolate with the cream in
the frying dish.
The skewers can be grilled and then dipped
or eaten as is.

BRIQUETTES
x6

GRILLED PINEAPPLE WITH MALIBU SYRUP

Serves 4

1 medium pineapple
Honey
250ml sugar (8.7oz)
100ml water (3.5oz)
50ml Malibu coconut liquor (1.7oz)
60ml (8.7oz) toasted almond slivers/
toasted cashews

Prepare your Cobb with the frying dish.
Make a Malibu syrup by slowly bringing the
sugar and water to the boil and then boil for
about 8 minutes until syrupy.
Add the Malibu and bring to the boil again.
Cut the pineapple into four lengthways with
the skin on or off.
Grill on the Cobb griddle plate until golden
and at the end brush with honey and
caramelise.
Serve drizzled with Malibu syrup, toasted
almonds and a fruit sorbet or ice cream.

BRIQUETTES
x7

CARAMEL BANANAS ROASTED IN THEIR SKINS

Serves 4

4 large bananas
250g butter (0.5lbs)
500g castor sugar (1.1lbs)
500ml cream (17.5oz)
Vanilla ice cream
Toasted almonds

Prepare the Cobb with the roasting rack first, then get the fying dish ready.

Roast the banana on the roasting rack until the skin blackens and feels soft.

Place the frying dish on the Cobb.

Melt the butter and add the sugar into the frying dish, stirring constantly allowing the sugar to turn to a dark caramel colour (watch it does not burn).

Add the cream and bring the mixture to the boil again.

Make a slit lengthways in the skin of the cooked banana, top with lots of caramel sauce, a scoop of vanilla ice cream and the toasted almonds.

BRIQUETTES
x6

PANCAKES

2 eggs
200ml milk (7oz)
30ml oil (1oz)
5ml lemon juice or brandy (0.1oz)
250ml cake flour (8.7oz)
1ml salt (0.03oz)
150ml water (5.2oz)
Extra oil
Cinnamon sugar (Mixture of cinnamon
and castor sugar)
Golden syrup
Chocolate shavings

Mix eggs, milk, oil and lemon juice together.
Add flour and salt and mix until smooth.
Add water then allow to rest for 30 minutes.
Prepare the Cobb with the frying pan.
Lightly brush the surface with oil.
Pour a thin layer of mixture onto the pan.
As it sets, flip the pancake and bake it till light brown.
Sprinkle with cinnamon sugar and roll.
Top with a drizzle of syrup and chocolate shavings.

CHOCOLATE CAKE

Makes 1 x 20cm (8 inches) cake tin
75g butter (2.6oz)
100g sugar (3.5oz)
1 large egg
175g wheat flour (6.2oz)
1 1/2 (7.5ml) teaspoons baking powder (0.26oz)
2 tablespoons cocoa powder (1oz)
1 teaspoon vanilla essence (0.2oz)
100ml milk (3.5oz)
100g dark chocolate (3.5oz)
Ganache
250ml cream (8.7oz)
500g chocolate dark or medium (1.1lbs)

Cream the butter and sugar together and add
the egg, beating till pale.
Mix the flour, cocoa and vanilla essence together
and add to the butter mixture.
Melt the chocolate and stir into the cake mixture.
Pour into a well greased and lined 20cm (8 inches)
cake tin.
Prepare the Cobb with the roasting rack and
heat for 7 minutes with the lid on.
Place on the Cobb roasting rack, with the lid on
and bake for 40-50 minutes.
Once the sponge is ready change the roasting
rack to the frying dish.
To make the ganache bring the cream to the boil
in the frying dish and add chopped chocolate.
Remove from heat and stir until smooth.
Allow to thicken at room temperature.
Remove the cake from the pan and cool.
Cut in half, lengthways and spread with ganache.
Spread the rest of the ganache over the top and
decorate with lots of strawberries and
wafer biscuits.
Serve with a dollop of fresh cream or crème
fraiche.

BRIQUETTES
x8

BBQ SAUCE

1 onion, chopped
1 cup tomato sauce (8.8oz)
100ml chutney (3.5oz)
100ml light brown sugar (3.5oz)
6ml paprika (0.2oz)
Juice of 1 lemon

Chop the onion and add the tomato sauce
and chutney.
Add the sugar, paprika and lemon juice.
No seasoning is added to the marinade so
that the meat may be seasoned later.
Use with meat or chicken.

JAMAICAN JERK MARINADE

1 medium onion, finely chopped
4 spring onions, finely chopped
1 chilli, finely chopped
3 tablespoons soy sauce (1.6oz)
1 tablespoon oil (0.5oz)
1 tablespoon white vinegar (0.5oz)
2 teaspoons fresh thyme (0.3oz)
2 teaspoons sugar (0.3oz)
1 teaspoon salt (0.2oz)
1 teaspoon Allspice, ground (0.2oz)
1 teaspoon black pepper, ground (0.2oz)
1/2 teaspoon nutmeg, ground (0.08oz)
1/2 teaspoon cinnamon, ground (0.08oz)

Combine all ingredients in a blender and blend
until smooth.
This marinade can be stored in the refrigerator
for up to one month.
This goes best with chicken but would also
go well with fish.
Coat the chicken with the marinade and cook,
basting as you go.

SATAY MARINADE

1 tablespoon light brown sugar (0.5oz)
1 tablespoon curry powder (0.5oz)
2 tablespoons crunchy peanut butter (1oz)
1/2 cup soy sauce (4.4oz)
1/2 cup freshly squeezed lime juice (4.4oz)
2 Garlic cloves, minced
Crushed dried chillies

Mix together and use to marinate chicken or
pork.
Marinate for 30 minutes then sauté the meat.
Drizzle with fresh lime juice to taste.

THAI MARINADE

2 red chillies
1 garlic clove
15ml castor sugar (0.5oz)
15ml lime juice (0.5oz)
45ml fish sauce (1.5oz)
15ml rice wine vinegar (0.5oz)
60ml olive oil (2.1oz)
30ml white wine vinegar (1oz)
15ml fresh coriander, chopped (0.5oz)

Mix ingredients together and blend lightly in
a blender.
Good for fish, pork or chicken.

SAUTÉ POTATOES

Serves 4
4 medium potatoes
250g streaky bacon (0.5lbs)
1 onion, sliced
2 cloves garlic, crushed
Handful parsley
Salt and pepper

Thinly slice or cut the potatoes in 1.5cm dice.
Prepare the Cobb with the frying dish.
Heat for 5 minutes with the lid on.
Chop the bacon and fry until crisp.
Remove the bacon and in the same frying
dish, fry the onions until golden.
Remove the onions from the frying dish and
once again in the same frying dish, fry the
potatoes until golden and cooked through.
Add all the other ingredients to the frying dish
and season.
Sprinkle with fresh parsley.
Eat as an accompaniment to meat or with
breakfast.

CUCUMBER AND CORIANDER RAITA

250ml Greek yoghurt (8.7oz)
150ml (5.2oz) cucumber, cubed with seeds
removed
Small handful Coriander leaves, chopped
roughly
Juice of 1/2 lemon
3ml sugar (0.1oz)
Salt and pepper

Mix the cucumber with the yoghurt.
Add the chopped coriander.
Season with the other ingredients.
Serve with chicken or meat as well as
hamburgers.

STIR FRY

800g (01.8lbs) stir fry mix or cut your own
julienne vegetables (carrots, cabbage, mixed
peppers, baby marrow, aubergine, spinach
and onion)
20ml olive oil (0.7oz)
30ml soy sauce (1oz)
Squeeze of lemon
10ml honey (0.3oz)
10ml sesame oil (0.3oz)
Handful chopped coriander
Salt and pepper

Prepare the Cobb with the frying dish and
heat for 7 minutes (till very hot) with
the lid on.
Add oil and quickly stir fry the vegetables in
2 batches, remove the first and repeat so that
the vegetables remain crisp.
Add the 2 batches together.
Add the soy sauce, lemon, honey, sesame,
coriander and seasoning.
Goes well with fish and chicken and can be
used in the Fish en Papilotte pouch.

STUFFED MUSHROOMS

Serves 4
8 big black mushrooms
400g cous-cous salad (14oz)
200g grated mozzarella (7oz)
50g feta crumbled (1.7oz)
50ml pesto (basil) (1.7oz)
Salt and pepper
Rocket leaves or basil
50 ml olive oil (1.7oz)
25 ml balsamic vinegar (10.8oz)

Remove stems, peel and brush the mushrooms
with olive oil.
Fill the cup of the mushroom with cous-cous
salad, top with grated mozzarella.
Prepare the Cobb with the roasting rack
and heat.
Place the mushrooms on the roasting rack for
8-10 minutes with the lid on.
Crumble feta over the top, season and drizzle
with pesto. Top with rocket leaves tossed in
balsamic vinegar and olive oil. Makes a good
vegetarian meal.